Pet Care

A DOG FOR YOU

Caring for Your Dog

Written by Susan Blackaby

Illustrated by Charlene DeLage

Content Advisers: Jennifer Zablotny, D.V.M.,
Kerrie Burns, D.V.M.

Reading Adviser: Susan Kesselring, M.A., Literacy Educator
Rosemount-Apple Valley-Eagan (Minnesota) School District

PICTURE WINDOW BOOKS
Minneapolis, Minnesota

Editor: Nadia Higgins
Designer: Nathan Gassman
Page production: Picture Window Books
The illustrations in this book were painted with watercolor.

Picture Window Books
5115 Excelsior Boulevard
Suite 232
Minneapolis, MN 55416
1-877-845-8392
www.picturewindowbooks.com

Printed in the United States of America.
1 2 3 4 5 6 08 07 06 05 04 03

Library of Congress Cataloging-in-Publication Data
Blackaby, Susan.
A dog for you : caring for your dog / written by Susan Blackaby ; illustrated by Charlene DeLage.
v. cm. — (Pet care)
Contents: You and your dog—Food and shelter—Safe and sound—Fit and trim—Clean, healthy, and happy—Make
a dog-eared dictionary—Fun facts—It takes all kinds.
ISBN 1-4048-0114-6 (lib. bdg.)
1. Dogs—Juvenile literature. [1. Dogs.] 1. DeLage, Charlene, 1944- ill. II. Title.
SF427 .B545 2003
636.7'0887—dc21
2002155004

TABLE OF CONTENTS

You and Your Dog

Dogs come in all shapes and sizes.

Some dogs are big.

Some dogs are little.

Some dogs are long, and some are short.

Most dogs make fine friends.

In the wild, dogs live in packs.

One dog is the leader.

In your home, *you* are the top dog.

Your dog knows that you are in charge.

Training will help your dog behave and be safe.

Teach your dog to sit, lie down, walk on a leash, and come to you.

Your dog will quickly learn how to make you happy.

Food and Shelter

Feed your dog at the same time each day.

Give it lots of fresh water.

Hand out healthy treats when your dog is extra good.

Some food can make a dog as sick as a dog.

Do not let your dog eat:

- 🐾 Chocolate
- 🐾 Garbage
- 🐾 Grapes and raisins
- 🐾 Houseplants
- 🐾 Macadamia nuts
- 🐾 Mushrooms
- 🐾 Onions
- 🐾 Raw meat
- 🐾 Sharp bones

Your dog needs a safe place to sleep.

A dog can nap in a crate.

It can doze in a basket.

Your dog can snooze on a rug.

It can curl up with you.

Safe and Sound

Make a safe, clean spot for your dog to stay.

On hot days, your dog needs shade.

On wet days, your dog needs to get out of the rain.

On cold days, your dog needs a cozy corner.

Fit and Trim

Do not let your dog get out of shape!

Give your dog lots of fresh air and exercise.

Let your dog romp in your yard.

Take your dog for walks.

Be sure to clean up after your dog.

Your dog can have fun on or off the leash.

Some parks have places for dogs to play.

When is it OK to let your dog run free?

🐾 It is legal to take your dog off the leash.

🐾 You are in a safe place.

🐾 Your dog cannot run away.

🐾 Your dog comes every time you call.

Clean, Healthy, and Happy

Keep your dog clean, and your dog will be healthy and happy.

Trim your dog's toenails.

Check your dog's ears and teeth.

Brush your dog to keep it from shedding too much fur.

Most indoor dogs shed all the time.

Outdoor dogs shed mostly in the fall and spring.

Your dog needs a checkup every year.

The vet will make sure your dog is OK.

The vet will give your dog the shots it needs to stay healthy.

When to call the vet:

- Your dog is sick.
- Your dog is hurt.
- Your dog will not eat.
- Your dog has no pep.

Your dog needs just one more thing.

Your dog needs oodles of love from you.

Make a Dog-eared Dictionary

There are many words and phrases in English that have to do with dogs. For instance, *dog-eared* means something that is shabby or worn. It comes from books that look worn out after people turned down the pages at the corner, making the corners look like a dog's ears.

Draw pictures to go with these doggy sayings.

Let sleeping dogs lie.

I'd like a doggie bag, please.

It is a dog's life.

He is a lucky dog.

You cannot teach an old dog new tricks.

Fun Facts

 Foxes, wolves, and coyotes are in the dog family.

 People in the Stone Age trained dogs to help them hunt.

 A Russian dog named Laika went up in space before any people did.

 Dogs have 42 teeth.

 A greyhound can run 45 miles (72 kilometers) per hour.

Words to Know

checkup—a visit to the vet to make sure your dog is healthy

pack—a group of wolves that lives together

shed—to lose hair

vet (short for veterinarian)—a doctor who treats animals

It Takes All Kinds

The American Kennel Club lists 150 kinds, or breeds, of dogs. They divide the dogs into seven groups. A dog's group can tell you about the dog's looks and how it acts.

Dog Group — Breed

Dog Group	Breed
Toy (small dogs)	Chihuahua, Toy Poodle, Pug, Pekingese, Yorkshire Terrier
Terrier (very active dogs, often with wiry fur)	Airedale, Jack Russell Terrier, Fox Terrier, Miniature Schnauzer
Non-sporting (large dogs, not used for hunting)	Boston Terrier, Bulldog, Dalmatian, Poodle
Sporting (hunting dogs, energetic and easy to train)	Pointer, Labrador Retriever, Golden Retriever, Cocker Spaniel
Hound (gentle dogs, known either for their terrific sense of smell or sight)	Basset Hound, Beagle, Bloodhound, Dachshund, Irish Wolfhound
Working (big and strong, often used as guard dogs)	Boxer, Newfoundland, St. Bernard, Husky
Herding (dogs used by farmers to gather sheep or cows)	Australian Shepherd, Border Collie, German Shepherd, Old English Sheepdog

To Learn More

At the Library

Altman, Linda Jacobs. *Big Dogs*. New York: Benchmark, 2001.

Brown, Marc. *Arthur's New Puppy*. Boston: Little, Brown, and Company, 1997.

Frost, Helen. *Dogs*. Mankato, Minn.: Pebble Books, 2000.

George, Jean Craighead. *How to Talk to Your Dog*. New York: HarperCollins, 2000.

Graham, Bob. *"Let's Get a Pup!" Said Kate*. Cambridge, Mass.: Candlewick, 2001.

On the Web

ASPCA Kids' Site

http://www.animaland.org

For stories, games, and information about pets

American Kennel Club

http://www.akc.org

For fun information about dog breeds and dog care

Want to learn more about dogs? Visit FACT HOUND at *http://www.facthound.com*.

Index